ANIMAL ILLUMINATION

ANIMAL ILLUMINATION

The Essential Guide to Learning
Intuitive Animal Communication

Ingrid M. Brammer

iUniverse, Inc.
Bloomington

Animal Illumination
The Essential Guide to Learning Intuitive Animal Communication

iUniverse books may be ordered through booksellers or by contacting:

iUniverse
1663 Liberty Drive
Bloomington, IN 47403
www.iuniverse.com
1-800-Authors (1-800-288-4677)

Because of the dynamic nature of the Internet, any web addresses or links contained in this book may have changed since publication and may no longer be valid. The views expressed in this work are solely those of the author and do not necessarily reflect the views of the publisher, and the publisher hereby disclaims any responsibility for them.

Any people depicted in stock imagery provided by Thinkstock are models, and such images are being used for illustrative purposes only.

Certain stock imagery © Thinkstock.

ISBN: 978-1-4502-9327-3 (sc)
ISBN: 978-1-4502-9328-0 (ebook)

Printed in the United States of America

iUniverse rev. date: 02/17/2011

To my horses and animals,

For awakening and illuminating my life;

*And with love and gratitude to my Spiritual Mentor and
cherished friend, Fay Mansfield,*

*For guiding me on my journey and exploration to all things
possible.*

Table of Contents

Preface

Animal communication is a beautiful life-altering gift that is available to *anyone* with an open heart and mind. As an animal lover and a person with many pets, I first came upon the concept of animal communication with open enthusiasm and eagerness to learn. However, after working in the computer sciences for twenty-five years, the analytical side of me wanted to know more. I wanted to understand how animal communication was possible, how I was achieving unbelievable results, and what exactly was going on. What has transpired in my life since the initial start several years ago has been truly life changing; you can even say that the animals have truly illuminated me.

It is my intention with this book and my workshops to share this discovery with you. My greatest hope is that it may become the start of a new journey for you, opening doors that were never before revealed, for the betterment of all living creatures.

This book is laid out in two sections:

Section One: "Base Foundation" provides an explanation of intuitive animal communication, how it works, and some of the science behind it. You do not have to understand it to be successful, but I find it is helpful for most students.

Section Two: "How to Communicate Intuitively with Animals" provides the detailed steps to learn and practice intuitive communication with animals.

This guide is compact, yet thorough and concise, with explanations to get you started quickly on your journey of success.

Blessings,

Ingrid

Introduction

I was patiently awaiting the birth of our first foal, sleeping in the barn not to miss the moment. I was grateful to witness the whole event and be there for my mare should she need any help. It went flawlessly and we had our first little colt. It took less than an hour for Galeon to find his wobbly legs and make his way over to me sitting in a lawn chair at the opening of the stall door. He slowly raised his head to smell my face and proceeded to try to find a drink of milk on my ear lobe. From that moment I was in love! For the next 4 years Galeon and I have continued to have a strong link and he looks to me for guidance and comfort when scary situations appear, like the tractor that was moved a few feet over from where it was yesterday. I hear his thoughts very clearly and can respond to settle him down.

In the summer of 2010, as a 4 year old it was Galeon's big day to go off to training and learn to be under saddle. It was a big moment for him as he needed to learn how to load and travel on the trailer and be away from his herd and family. I helped to prepare his mind by talking to him and explaining what was going to happen and what to expect.

I told him that he was going away for a couple of months to learn how to work like his Dad. He was going to come back home once he was fully trained and I was not abandoning him as he was being entrusted to someone that he already knew, a natural horsemanship professional Annie Lalande.

I told him to make me very proud and to listen and learn from Annie as she had much to teach him. Once we arrived at the farm I introduced him to some of the other horses including 2 he had known from the past and explained how and when he knew them.

The next day I went to visit to reinforce I had not abandoned him and to see how he settled in. He was in the single paddock in the back of the arena by himself with the gelding herd on one side of the fence and the mare herd on the other. He stood looking at the mares to be as close to them as possible. I asked him if he had met the boys on the other side and if he wanted to introduce them to me. He turned before I could make a movement and started to lead me over to the boys' side. They all came over and everyone smelled noses and I explained to him that he was going to be in with them in a day or two. He had a huge sigh, then a snort of release and with tension relieved began grazing alongside the fence.

During the week I tuned in from home several times to see how he was doing. The first thoughts were very clear as he was telling me "You would be so proud of me Mom. I started working and I am learning very quickly". I went to visit him a few days later and watched him work and Annie said to me "I am very proud of him, he is learning very quickly." She also mentioned that he has such beautiful movement. After the lesson Annie and I were brushing Galeon and I was telling her the story of his Dad, Diestro and how he would take care of me and keep me safe in the winter when the ice came off the arena roof. You will read more on that story later in the book. Little did I know Galeon was listening to our full conversation as the next example clearly shows.

One of my students and very good friend Sarah had asked

me how Galeon was doing. Telling her nothing, I instead asked her to tune in and talk to him and see what he tells her. Here is the result:

"As soon as I tuned into him his head popped up and he spun around like he is so happy to be talking to me, like an excited little boy! He tells me he is a big boy now, he's proud to be learning and training and he can't believe what he can do and how much he is learning. He wonders if I know that he's away from his Mom for the first time, like far away for the first time, he is thinking about his friends but he knows he's coming back. He can't wait to show off what he has learned, he says he is beautiful and he feels like he can float, he wants to show off what he knows and what he has learned. He's like a little boy that is all excited to go to school for the first time and is all dressed up and proud of himself... he's feeling really good. He also made me believe that he wants to be your horse, he wants you to ride him and he will take care of you. He wants to prove to you that he can do it and he will take care of you, he just kept saying that he would take care of you if you ride him."

The next day Sarah wrote me again with the following update:

"I was sitting at home and kept getting side tracked with questions from Galeon... it was very strange, it was like he wouldn't let me work (can I ask you something, can I talk to you for a minute). He's worried about the saddle and the rider part; he doesn't know what to do. I explained it all to him and what he needs to do and just to worry about keeping his balance and keeping all 4 feet on the ground. Strange but he seemed to be asking me if I could run through it with him and explain it to him. He seems to be nervous about getting a person up there and what it is going to feel like, what will he do... so very strange that he just kept coming through so strong for about 5 minutes... he's thanking me now!"

I realized I was so worried with him leaving the farm that

I didn't even explain anything about the saddle and what to expect. I was glad Sarah was there to help him through it.

Helping your animals through change starts with the knowing that they can understand us and that they look to us for guidance and explanation. Change is scary for all living beings and with a little upfront explanation it can help take some of the stress out of the situation.

This is just one of the many possibilities that having an understanding of the fundamental aspects of animal communication can lead to. We will explore how this is possible, alongside examples and through practice provide you the fundamentals to get you on your journey.

Section 1:
Base Foundation

What is Animal Communication?

Animals naturally have the ability to talk to each other; for them it is a survival mechanism and a way of life. They do this through *telepathy*, by sending and receiving thoughts, feelings, and messages.

Horses and other herd animals are good examples of how animals use telepathy with each other and within the herd. Linda Kohanov writes in her book, *The Tao of Equus*, that one day, while sitting in the field, reading, her horse, Noche, spotted something that scared him. At the moment he saw it, a shockwave of fear hit Linda. All the other horses in the herd looked up to see what the danger was. Linda looked over and saw a mountain biker riding on a path. His helmet looked like an alien's head; his bike was also reflecting the sun, and she thought it would certainly be a strange and startling sight for these horses. She then laughed, and as the horses felt her calmness, they too calmed down and went back to their grazing.

I have experienced similar situations with my own horses. I am now so tuned in with my horses that I can sense when they are going to be silly or spooked, or when they are going to jump or act out, before they actually do. Many people who experience this don't realize that they are communicating with their natural intuitive abilities.

Animals have never been told that they can't do something, or that they are "making it up," that "it is impossible," or they are "just being silly." For them, using telepathy is normal. No one mocks them for this natural ability.

In one study reported by Lynne McTaggart, in *The Field*, she explains that ants were studied under special equipment that displayed their energy in the form of light. The scientists witnessed a light being passed from one ant to the other, in which it appeared they were communicating with each other.

Animals also have the ability to talk interspecies. They communicate with people; not only can they send us messages, but they can also read our minds. In the book, *Dogs That Know When Their Owners Are Coming Home,* by Rupert Sheldrake, he provides examples that explain this concept.

> *Kate Laufer, a midwife and social worker in Solbergmeon, Norway, works at odd hours and returns home at unexpected times, but whenever her husband, Walter, is home, he greets her with a hot cup of freshly brewed tea. What accounts for her husband's uncanny timing? The family dog, Tiki, the terrier. "When Tiki rushes to the window and stands on the windowsill," says Walter Laufer, "I know that my wife is on her way home."*
>
> *When the telephone rings in the household of a noted professor at the University of California in Berkeley, his wife knows when her husband is on the other end of the line. How? Whiskins, the family's silver tabby cat rushes to the telephone and paws at the receiver. "Many times he succeeds in taking it off the hook and makes appreciative meows that are clearly audible to my husband at*

the other end," she says "If someone else telephones, Whiskins takes no notice."

Sheldrake conducted several experiments and interviews to prove that indeed animals do connect with us regardless of distance and time, and sense what is going on with their people. In one case, the dog picked up the thoughts and intentions of the owner before his journey started.

This was the case with Frank Harrison, who was taken ill soon after he joined the British Army and on his discharge from the hospital, was given a few days' sick leave. He did not inform his parents.

"When I arrived home Sandy, our Irish Terrier, was by the door and I was told that he had not moved from the door for two days, except to be fed and exercised. This was about the time I had been told I was being given sick leave. His behavior had naturally caused concern to my parents. When I unexpectedly arrived home my mom said, 'He knew you were coming. That explains it.' This waiting at the door happened throughout my two and a half years of service in the army, Sandy would move to the door about forty-eight hours before I came home. My parents knew I was coming home, because Sandy knew."

Humans are also born with this ability; however, we stop using it as we grow out of childhood. Many well- known psychics who claim that they have had their skills since they were born, either had some type of encouragement to hone those skills, or chose not to listen to naysayers and continued to nurture their abilities. The rest of us have been taught to ignore our natural ability and around age seven, we began to turn off and ignore our intuitive capabilities, as this was more socially acceptable.

Many aborigines and other tribes around the globe continue to use this ability, as it is cherished and encouraged within their tribes. Many traditions and rituals are based on personal intuitive ability, such as the vision quest, which is a spiritual journey undertaken as a rite of passage, or as a personal search for guidance, typically seen in Native American culture.

It is never too late to re-activate it; all you need is:

- ♥ the understanding and knowledge about intuitive abilities
- ♥ the will and intention to learn
- ♥ the belief that you have the ability
- ♥ plenty of practice

How Does Animal Communication Work?

According to *Webster's Online Dictionary:* **Telepathy** (literally "distant perception/feeling") comes from the Greek *tele*, meaning "distant," and *pathe*, meaning "feeling." It refers to the supposed ability to communicate information from one mind to another, and is one form of extra-sensory perception or anomalous cognition. This information is generally reported as being "received" in the same form as that from the conventional senses. Other names for this can be: sixth sense, intuition, and psychic ability.

To understand telepathy, let's compare it to a wireless cell network. The cell phone runs on a certain frequency that other cell phones and cell towers can hear and transmit. We cannot see it, but we know it works when we pick up the phone and hear the other person. The phone acts as a tuner, amplifier, or antenna.

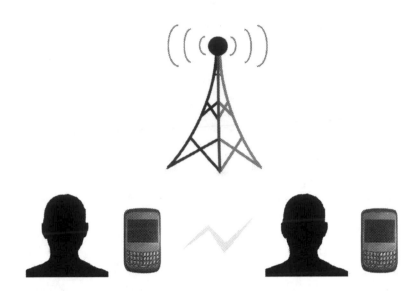

With people, it is the same process. Our thoughts and feelings are a form of energy, which is sent out to others, and if you have your "tuner" on, you can receive it. This is not limited to people, but all energy forms, including animals, plants, and nature. *Everything* has energy.

A great example of this was documented in the book, *The Secret Life of Plants*, by Peter Tompkins. He describes the story of Cleve Backster, a lie-detector examiner with the CIA, who discovered that plants appeared to be sentient. In 1966, when Backster was working late one evening, he decided to attach the electrodes of the lie detector machine to the leaf of a dracaena, or a dragon tree. He wanted to see the effects after watering the plant. He expected the meters to trend upward, but instead they went downward, due to the greater electrical conductivity of the moister plant. He felt that the plant reacted similarly to a human being who experienced an emotional stimulus.

He then decided to focus on experimenting with an emotional stimulus. With humans, the best way to do this is to threaten their wellbeing. So he tried that theory with the plant by dipping a leaf in a cup of hot coffee. Without seeing much of a reaction, he wondered if the threat needed to be larger, so he thought he should burn the leaf that the electrodes were attached to, with a match or lighter. At the time of that thought, Backster had not moved or attempted anything, but the tracing pattern on the graph of the recording machine began to have a dramatic change, in the form of a prolonged upward sweep of the recording pen. It appeared that the plant had picked up Backster's thoughts.

Additional studies were done for several years by other scientists that proved the phenomenon.

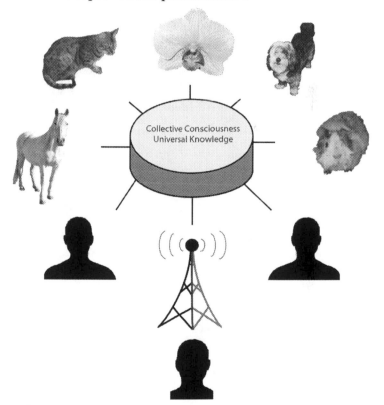

There are several terms that have been used to recognize the form of united energy that we all share:

♥ Collective Consciousness, as described by Swiss Psychologist Carl Jung

♥ Universal Knowledge

♥ Universal Energy

♥ God, Buddha, Jehovah, Creator, Divine, etc., as described by many religions and belief systems

♥ Quantum Physics, as known by scientists

Quantum Physics

Quantum Physics states that all matter and energy is interconnected and potentially entangled, and neither distance nor time separates us. This definition didn't really help me understand how that translated to animal communication, so I continued my research to make sense of it all. These definitions helped:

The *atom* is a basic unit of matter, which, at the center is a nucleus surrounded by negatively charged electrons. The nucleus contains positively charged protons and electrically neutral neutrons.

Within the atom, physicists have discovered subatomic components and structures. Quantum mechanics looks at the subatomic components (electrons, protons, and even smaller particles - Quarks).

The subatomic particles inside atoms wiggle and produce a vibration that gives off light and other electromagnetic radiation. Bursts of light are called *photons*. The frequency of the vibration determines the energy it gives off.

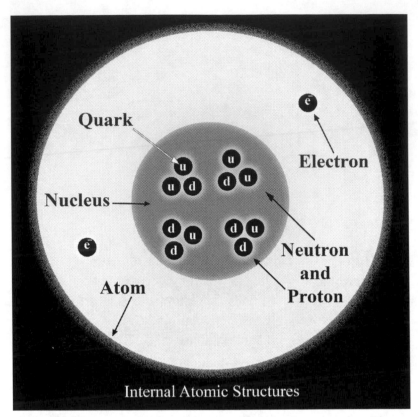

Internal Atomic Structures

It was a struggle for me to understand quantum theory until I found the book, *The Intention Experiment*, by Lynne McTaggart. Her first book, *The Field*, further explained the foundation. McTaggart is an investigative reporter who embarked on a journey to understand how *distance energy healing* worked, and interviewed many scientists in the process. She needed the explanations in laymen's terms so she, herself, could understand and write about it. She explains these elements that helped me put it together in my own mind.

Subatomic particles resemble little packets of vibrating waves that pass energy back and forth, as if in an endless game of basketball. These back and forth passes, which rise to great states of energy, are known collectively as the *zero point field.* The field is called "zero point" because even at the temperature of absolute zero (−460 degrees Fahrenheit), when all matter theoretically should stop moving, these tiny fluctuations are still detectable. Even at the coldest place in the universe, subatomic matter never comes to rest, but carries on this little energy tango.

If all matter in the universe was interacting with the zero point field, it meant, quite simply, that all matter was interconnected and potentially entangled throughout the cosmos. And if we, and all of empty space, are a mass of entanglement, we must be establishing invisible connections with things at a distance from ourselves. Acknowledging the existence of the zero point field and entanglement, offers a ready mechanism for why signals being generated by the power of thought can be picked up by someone else many miles away.

McTaggart also cites a study conducted by Gary Schwartz, a scientist who studied the light energy emitted from healers' hands, using something called a CCD camera.

Schwartz had witnessed just this coherent photon stream emanating from the hands of the healers. He finally had his answer about the source of healing. He concluded that if thoughts are generated as frequencies, healing intention is well-ordered light.

The speed of light is 186,000 miles per second. Therefore if the Earth's circumference is 24,901.55 miles, then light can travel around the earth over 7 times in one second.

This highlighted to me that our connection to the zero point field and the subatomic particles of matter, which is vibrating and producing energy or light, is the highway that allows our thoughts to travel. Our thoughts, our connection to another consciousness (either person or animal) can happen regardless of distance because we can connect in milliseconds.

When connecting with an animal we connect our heart centers together and this is a form of Quantum entanglement.

Energy and Auras

We all have an energy field called an *aura*. We cannot see it, but we can feel it. Kirlian photography can photograph your aura. Your aura energy will change with your emotions, your environment, and your health.

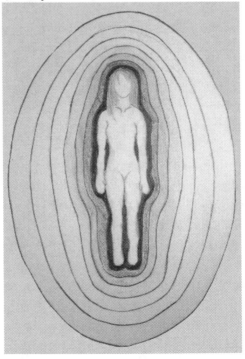

It is my belief that animals and babies can either see or sense our auras. Often children will draw shade around people with various colors when they are creating pictures.

A person's aura is about eight to ten feet around the body, with multiple layers. The aura of a healthy person, both physically and spiritually, is more vibrant and extends out further than someone who is unhealthy. The stronger your aura the more likely you will be able to fend off outside energy influences. Increasing your auric energy increases your telepathic abilities. Here are some simple things you can do to increase your awareness of auric energy:

Exercise 1: Place your hands, palms facing each other, about eight inches apart. Slowly move your palms together until you can feel a resistance. This is your energy field.

Exercise 2: Have someone sit in a chair. From behind walk toward the chair with your palms facing the person, and notice once you sense the person's aura. The person in the chair should also tell you when they feel you in their aura. You can try this with your animals as well. It is an excellent exercise to work with horses because they tell you through their body language the moment you touch their energy layer.

Exercise 3: Ask a person to sit in a chair while you stand approximately ten feet away. Take two ordinary metal hangers and hold them in your hands lightly so they can easily move on their own. Ask out loud for the hangers to show you the aura of the person in the chair, and then walk slowly toward them. When you reach the edge of the person's aura the hangers will move outward. You can also ask where someone is in the room and they will move and point to the person. You may also feel the energy in the hangers as they try to move.

This is an example that our thoughts are a form of energy, which is a useful tool in animal communication. Animals read and feel our energy and we can learn to read and feel theirs.

Chakras

We have energy centers in our body, called *chakras*, that allow the energy to flow. Each chakra operates at a different frequency, and has its own vibration. Ideally, when chakras are open and balanced, harmony exists in the body. In this state, the individual is best prepared for intuitive communication.

To enhance your energy vibrations (which will increase your ability to communicate with animals) you need to work on opening these energy centers.

Each chakra is associated with specific areas of the human condition.

The following list describes what each chakra represents:

Crown – where we connect to the universal energy; wisdom and understanding

Third Eye – intuition, perception

Throat – communication

Heart – feelings, emotions, love, compassion

Solar Plexus – power and will

Sacral – desire

Root – grounding, survival, protection

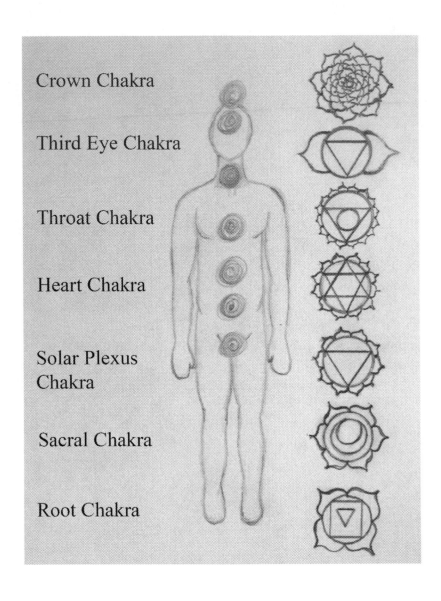

Crown Chakra

Third Eye Chakra

Throat Chakra

Heart Chakra

Solar Plexus
Chakra

Sacral Chakra

Root Chakra

The chakra colors are the same as those of the rainbow and also those of a crystal.

When you shine white light through a crystal prism, you can see the chakra colors refract through the crystal.

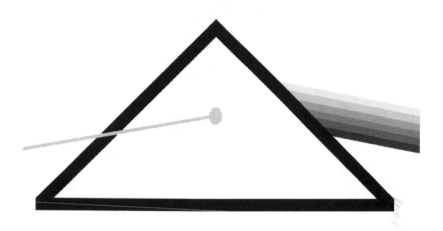

Exercise: Try sitting and visualizing a bright white light entering through the top of your head and opening each chakra, like little doors, with the corresponding color for each chakra.

Brain Activity

Delta waves .5 – 4 cycles per second (Hz)	Sleep (deep dreamless or dreaming sleep). During birth to 2 years of age this is the primary state.
Theta waves 4-8 Hz	Drowsy idealing, just before falling asleep. During ages of 2 to 6 years this is the primary state.
Alpha waves 8-12 Hz	Calm Consciousness / Relaxed Reflecting / Awareness States of brainstorming, innovation, creative activity and Animal communication.
Beta waves 12-35 Hz	Alert, Working. Starting at 12 years of age we stay in this state most of the time. Working, thinking, sometimes stressed.
Gamma waves >35 Hz	Peak Performance - When all areas of the brain connect.

Most people exist with their brains in the beta wave state, which is the one associated with thought and activity. Our minds are consumed with to-do lists, work, school, relationships, finances, household chores, etc.

It is essential to slow down and quiet the mind to reach a calm state before attempting animal communication. This can be done by breathing exercises, meditations, or other quiet, focused exercises. The word *meditation* is often tarnished with social stereotypes and images of hippies or gurus humming the mantra, Om. But meditating is simply a method of silencing the mind, and it is increasingly being recognized as an essential part of a healthy lifestyle, especially when we are inundated with activities, stress, and various distractions.

It is no wonder that people are not in tune with their telepathy and intuition anymore. We never leave the beta state unless we are going to sleep. It is essential to slow down to the alpha wave to be in a state of awareness and relaxation. This state puts us into a more peaceful state of mind, and ultimately to *inner* peace. We require this in order to hear the messages that are coming to us. Essentially, we need to get out of our own way.

Children stay in the lower brain waves, which allow them to be in tune with their intuition. At age seven they move into the alpha waves, and by then, social influences begin to inhibit their natural curiosity about intuition. It isn't until we are twelve years old that our brains start to live in the beta waves.

Gamma waves are achieved by everyone at all ages when the brain is hard at work, focused on one specific problem or complex operation. Studies have shown that more of the brain functions turn on during this state. When in deep meditation (or, in this case, when doing an animal communication reading) a person will go from an alpha to a gamma state for focused connection.

The brain is made up of the left and right side. The left hemisphere controls logical or analytical thought, while the right is more creative and intuitive. We need both sides balanced, but typically one side is a little stronger than the other. Practicing intuitive studies and animal readings will increase the activity on the right side of the brain.

Jill Bolt Taylor, a Harvard-trained brain scientist, in her book, *My Stroke of Insight*, explains what happened to her when she had a stroke and the left side of her brain stopped working. She couldn't remember anything concrete, such as language or past events, and she didn't worry about the future. She lived in "the now" and lost all her worry and stress. Without her past, she had no baggage.

While this was an unfortunate event for Taylor, she claims that tapping into the right side of her brain was a life-changing experience for her. The stroke opened up a world unknown to her as a scientist . . . that of "living in the moment," which now influences the way she lives since her recovery.

Many studies have been done on the brain to understand what happens during "spiritual experiences," and they have proven that certain parts of the brain activate, particularly the frontal lobes.

Intuition

Intuition is a form of extrasensory perception (ESP). "Psychic" is another term; however this word often carries a negative stereotype. Intuition can also be called our "sixth sense," although it actually mirrors our five physical senses. There are a number of ways for intuition to manifest. Each acts as a kind of portal for communication.

Clairvoyance: In the same way you see with your physical eyes, clairvoyance allows you to see with your mind's eye. This form of intuition will bring visual pictures and movies that are similar to what you may have in your dreams.

Clairaudience: In the same way you hear with your ears, clairaudience allows you to hear with your *inner* ears. Messages may be in the form of words or sentences, and will often be in your own voice. Practicing your clairaudient skills will give you a clear understanding of whether the words you hear are coming from your animal friends or from your own mind.

Clairsentience: This form involves the ability to sense feelings and emotions. This can involve feeling physical pain or other physical feelings. You can ask to not feel pain and to relate the information in a different form. Often, animals will express their emotions to help you understand what is going on with them. You may feel them through clairsentience.

Clairalience: This form of intuition involves the ability to smell. This is typically experienced only in unique situations. It should be practiced by asking specific questions that will elicit a response involving the sense of smell.

Clairambience: This form is the ability to intuitively sense taste. This is another form that is not often experienced and should be practiced by asking questions that will elicit a response involving the sense of taste.

The final form of intuition can accompany any of the senses above.

Claircognizance: The intuitive person also has the ability to know information automatically, often appearing very quickly in one's thoughts. This can come with the visual pictures and then a knowing of what they mean, or with the inner hearing of sounds or words and a knowing of the sounds.

Each person will use one or more of the senses naturally and can develop the ability for all the others.

Intuitive Exercise - Sensory Meditation

To determine which form of intuition is your strongest, take a few minutes to do the exercise below and then answer the questions that follow. This will help you when you begin animal communication because you will know where your strong points lie. Take particular note during this exercise of what feels the most "real" to you, as this will be important when answering the questions.

It is best to do this exercise as a guided meditation by having someone read it to you while you close your eyes. Alternatively, you can record it and listen to the playback with your eyes closed.

> *Start by closing your eyes and taking a few deep breaths. Breathe in . . . relax, and breathe out. Feel the breath enter your body, capture all the tension, and then release it as you breathe out.*
>
> *Breathe in again, deeply, hold for a second, and release. You are feeling more relaxed with each breath.*
>
> *Now watch your mind begin to clear, and watch*

as your thoughts become farther and farther away, until they are like clouds floating above you. Notice how easy it is to hear my voice and to listen without any effort at all. Notice how calm, peaceful, and safe you are.

Now visualize, or just imagine that you are walking down a beautiful forest path. The sun is shining above you; streams of light are flowing through the trees, touching the ground, spotting it with hundreds of different shades of earth. Notice how peaceful the forest is as the trees, ferns, and wild flowers gently sway in a small breeze; how the air itself seems to shimmer before your eyes. Notice the wildlife that is around you as you continue to walk along this path . . . deer, rabbits, little squirrels, and chipmunks are playfully searching for nuts and pinecones.

Listen as the nuts and berries drop from the trees and land on the soft earth with little thuds, the leaves and foliage around you rustling in the wind. Now hear the sound of rushing water as you realize there is a stream winding through the forest up ahead. Listen as the wild deer walk on fallen leaves and earth. Hear the amazing songbirds as they sing to one another in the canopy.

Take a deep breath now and smell the earth; breathe it deep into your lungs and notice the smell of pine needles and moss. As you continue walking notice the smell of lavender and wild flowers that are surrounding you. As you approach the stream ahead notice the smells of the water and the wet mossy, root-like scent of the wet earth.

Feel the life around you; there is a clearing in the canopy, which allows a bright stream of sunlight into the forest. Pause underneath it and as you stand in the large ribbon of sun, feel the sun warming your skin, and feel the breeze playfully tingling as it passes and swirls around you. Continue walking now and slowly approach the stream, as you get closer the sounds of water trickling over the rocks becomes clearer. Take off your shoes now and feel the cool earth beneath your feet, take one step into the stream and feel as the cold waters touch your skin and the sandy, muddy bottom squishes in-between your toes. Walk across now and keep going.

Soon you come to a clearing and notice a large beautiful tree beside a small calm crystal pond. Walk through the clearing, smelling the grass, feeling as it rubs against your legs and creates an itchy sensation as you pass. Pause under the tree and look up, and see small yellow fruit dappling its long branches. Reach out and feel the bark, the pulse of life beneath your fingertips.

Look up now and notice a perfectly ripe yellow lemon above you, reach out and pick it from its branch and lower it so you can examine it. It is perfectly formed, smooth with small dimples in its skin. Notice the shape, lift it up to your nose and smell the citrus skin. Begin to walk to the pond and wash the lemon off, cleaning away any dust that might have settled on it feeling the warm water on your hands and the lemon between your fingers. Hear the water as you splash and disturb the peaceful surface causing ripples to fill the entire pond.

Holding the lemon in your hands, press your thumbs deep into its flesh, and smell the intense burst of citrus that it releases. Slowly take some of the lemon's flesh and raise it to your mouth. Feel the juices trickle down your throat, so sour and lemony. Taste the lemon as you chew it, and feel it as you swallow it. Follow it with a nice sweet drink, cleansing your palate.

Now, take a moment to admire your surroundings. Notice the sense of peace and relaxation you are feeling.

Now begin to let this experience go, coming back to the here and now. Gently feeling your body in your chair, moving your fingers and hands, and when you're ready gently open your eyes and notice how refreshed, rejuvenated and wonderful you feel.

Sensory Meditation created by Charlotte Brammer, practicing Spiritual Psychotherapist and Hypnotherapist

Sensory Meditation Questionnaire Count the number of "yes" answers to the following questions:

1. Did you see the path?
2. Did you see the trees?
3. Could you see the sun streaming through the canopy and dappling the forest floor?
4. Could you see the ferns sway in the breeze?
5. Could you see the animals around you?
6. Could you hear the animals dropping the pinecones around you?
7. Could you hear the leaves rustling?
8. Could you hear the sound of the creek, of trickling water?
9. Could you hear the songs of the forest's birds around you?

10. Could you hear the animals as they walked through the forest?

11. Could you smell the earth?

12. Could you smell the pine needles?

13. Could you smell the lavender and wildflowers?

14. Could you smell the wet mossy, root-like scent of the wet earth?

15. Could you smell the lemon?

16. Could you feel the sun warming your skin?

17. Could you feel the breeze tingling your skin?

18. Could you feel the cold water on your skin?

19. Could you feel the itchy sensation that the grass made when you passed through it?

20. Could you feel the bark of the lemon tree?

21. Could you taste the lemon?

Each section represents a different form of intuitive skill. The category you had the most "yes" answers to is your primary form. Secondary forms have lower numbers.

Question numbers and their associative intuitions:
    1-5 Visual – Clairvoyance
    6-10 Auditory – Clairaudience
    11-15 Smelling – Clairalience
    16-20 Feeling – Clairsentience
    21 Tasting – Clairambience
    11-21 Kinesthetic, merely the different senses the body has.

If you experienced a sound or a taste that was not actually present, this could be a claircognizant experience, a form of knowing.

Section 2:
How to Communicate Intuitively with Animals

Sending Information

We send information continuously to our animals, whether we realize it or not. They pick up and listen to our thoughts. A lot of what we think about is of no interest to them, so they tune us out.

One day, I had to take my cat, Tasha, to the vet, so I was thinking to myself, *I wonder where the cat carrier is*. I obviously had a picture in my mind of the vet or just thought the words in my head. At this moment, my Spaniel, Elmo, got up from sleeping, went into the corner, and began shaking. I had not said anything out loud or even attempted to get the cat, but Elmo picked up on my thoughts. He reacted as if I was getting ready to take *him* to the vet.

Another example that proved to me animals are naturally intuitive, happened one winter morning when I was leading my one-year-old horse, Galeon, out to the paddock. He was walking calmly beside me, with his head low, smelling the ground. I looked over his shoulder and saw a trail of coyote tracks coming from the forest to the manure pile. So I thought to myself, *Oh, I guess that is where the coyotes come to check out the pile*. Galeon instantly threw his head up, arched his back in fear, and turned quickly to look over at the forest. At that exact moment, I received the clear clairaudient message,

"What?!" This was coming from Galeon. I immediately sent him calm energy and told him, "It's okay; there isn't any danger right now." He then calmed down and we continued our walk. Sometimes we have to be careful what we are thinking.

When we talk to our animals, it is very important to keep all communication positive. If you say to your dog, "Don't chew the shoes," you will be sending a picture of him chewing a shoe. He doesn't hear the word "don't." Instead, you need to say, "Please keep your chewing to your bones." He will then see himself chewing a bone.

Always visualize what you want your animals to do. When riding, often horses will spook in a certain spot. As the pair come to a spot where this typically occurs, the person will often start to worry and think, *Oh this is the spooky spot, I hope he doesn't spook.* The horse hears the person worry, picks up pictures in the person's head, and complies with what he is being told. He spooks! Instead, the rider should visualize them going through the spot calmly, and with complete relaxation. This method usually works amazingly well.

If you are a horse rider, you may have already experienced times when you've thought to yourself, *Maybe I should canter now,* and wham, into a canter your horse goes, before any aid may have even been offered!

You cannot use animal communication to "control" your animal, though. Your communication work must operate as a partnership. The process is similar to parenting, where you need to work on certain behaviors, and use positive rewards to make lasting changes.

There are four methods of sending information.

Verbally – This method of speaking out loud is the most common, and our companions get to know what words mean. We also send pictures when we speak, even if we don't realize it. When we are speaking to them, they are aware of it and receive the words and pictures, rather than tuning them out.

Mentally – This involves speaking to animals in our minds. Without using a voice, we tell them stories, or convey words or whole thoughts.

Visually – Visual communication can be in the form of images, pictures, and movies.

Emotionally – Sending feelings and emotions is a very effective way to transmit information to animals.

Some methods may come more naturally to you than others. With practice, you will become proficient in combining the last three for full impact.

I will often send emotions when working with my horses because they can spook easily. They seem to respond best to soothing words and images. Before I had my own farm, I boarded my horses at a farm that had an indoor arena. I would take my stallion, Diestro, into the arena and start him on the lunge line. There were usually other horses there, so I would be at one corner or end of the arena. He would sometimes have a bit too much energy, perhaps even spook, and start to run and buck, and scare some of the other horses. I would instantly send him a big bubble of calm energy that was soothing, peaceful, and full of love. Every time, without fail, he would drop his head, soften his back, and slow down. I found this technique useful when riding, too, even indoors, as winters in Canada mean sliding snow and ice off the roof, sending most horses bolting down the arena.

I send emotional messages daily when handling foals. I find that when they have a scary moment, they turn to me and see what I am thinking and feeling before they react. I send them calm energy, lowering and grounding both my energy and theirs. When I do this, they don't react to what startled them.

You do not have to be in the same location with the animal to communicate with them. In fact, sometimes it can even be a distraction. As we have the ability to connect with the animal through telepathy, it doesn't matter where they are or what they are doing. I have talked to animals in various places around the world.

Always send clear and simple thoughts. Animals can pick up on incongruent words, thoughts, and feelings, which can cause them to lose trust. If you are angry with your animal, but acting like you aren't, it will know you are lying. "Negative" emotions are okay if you say them and own them. As long as you are being honest, you can say, "I am feeling really angry right now." They will respect you if you are being authentic.

When you speak to an animal, you must believe that the messages are being received. The energy in your thoughts is real; animals are naturally telepathic and will pick them up. Sometimes they need time to listen, as they may have learned to tune you out.

Exercises

Here are some exercises to practice sending messages to your animal companion.

- ♥ Think of something you admire in your companion and send the compliment to your animal, silently, in your mind. Know that it is received.

- ♥ Open your heart center and send love and compassion. See it being received.

- ♥ Send an image of a treat in your hand, and see your animal eating it. Once s/he comes over, give her the treat. If at first s/he is not listening, send the message telepathically, then out loud, then give it to her. Over time, s/he will come to you right away, with only the silent message.

♥ Without any physical or verbal messages, send a thought to your dog that it is time for a walk. Send the upbeat emotions typically related to walking and see if s/he comes to you. You don't need to be in the same room. Sit quietly, send a picture of you getting ready, then leaving the house, and then doing what s/he typically does on his walk. Then take him for the walk.

♥ When going on your walk, visualize the route you are planning to take, send this message, and see if your dog turns before you.

♥ For any animal, take two bowls and put the exact same food in them. Send a message of which one the animal should go to, and then put them both down, apart from each other. Let the animal choose one of the bowls. Try this everyday and switch the order around to see if the animal goes to the one you intended.

♥ When you are away from home, try sending messages to your companion that you are on your way back. Have someone at home notice if the animal responds in some way. Try coming home at different times of the day.

♥ Hide your dog's favorite toy when s/he is not looking. Then when she comes into the room, send her the picture of where the toy is and see if s/he finds it. You can seal the toy in an air tight container to ensure they do not find the toy from smell.

Receiving Information

Animals are continuously sending us information. Oftentimes, we do pick up their thoughts, although we may not realize that the thoughts are coming from them. Have you ever thought, *I bet my dog has to go outside*? Chances are your dog sent you that information and it wasn't just the clock that prompted the thought.

Other times, messages can be more obvious. In 2007, I decided to geld my eight-year-old stallion, Diestro. He had produced some wonderful foals and although he was a valuable stallion, I wanted him to enjoy being with the herd. We had just built him a stallion paddock so he could be out all day. However, he could see the herd next to him, and when they went down the hill and out of sight, he panicked. He began acting out and losing weight, so I talked to him, and he said to me, "I just want to be a horse, and be with the rest of them. Why can't I?" So we made an appointment with a vet to have him gelded. Prior to leaving, my daughter told Diestro that if he changed his mind, to give us a clear sign by bowing down on his front knees so we could stop the procedure.

When he got off the trailer he was brought into the clinic barn and put in a stall next to a mare in heat. Needless to say, he was a little excited and he was very stressed from the trailer ride. Once in his stall, he went down on his two front knees and then got back up again. We all know now that he was bowing; however, my daughter thought he was merely trying to lie down. He then proceeded to get down on his knees again, stand up, and look at her. She still did not get it, so he did it a third time. Finally, she realized what was happening and couldn't believe she had missed this clear sign.

She told him that the procedure wasn't until the next morning, so he could sleep on it and confirm in the morning whether or not to cancel or go ahead with it. Both my daughter and I tuned in and talked to him separately and confirmed our notes that he did indeed "just want to be a horse." We went ahead with the procedure.

I am happy to say he is now with the herd, and primarily spends his time with my mare who is also the mother to his two sons. He is very happy and content.

Believe in What You Are Receiving

To receive information from animals, it is usually best to start with animals that you don't know. This makes it is easier to avoid censoring the information, which can happen when you are familiar with the animal. With an unknown, you will not impose any preconceived thoughts into the messages.

I once did a reading on a cat and she told me that she hates baths. Since this is common for cats, you could easily doubt the message and assume that you thought that up yourself, especially in a beginning reading. But don't dismiss anything. In this particular reading, the message was so strong that I knew I was not making it up in my own mind.

I have done readings on many cats and not one has ever said it didn't like water. Later, when talking to the cat's person, she told me that she'd only had the cat for two months and it had a skin problem and had to bathe it regularly with medicated shampoos to clear up the condition.

Do not censor and do not interpret. Simply take everything you receive and write it down. With lots of practice you will experience just about everything, having confirmation is the key to believing.

Start a Journal

When I first started animal communications, I did hundreds of them, and I learned and experienced many things. I only asked for confirmation as a way to learn what I was picking up and how to interpret it. The best way to grow in this endeavor is to start a journal where you track all of your experiences.

Forms of Receiving

Referring back to the forms of intuition, you will receive information in one or more ways, including:

- ♥ **Visually** – seeing images, pictures, movies
- ♥ **Hearing** – hearing words, phrases, sounds
- ♥ **Feeling** – sensing emotions, feelings, pain

♥ **Knowing** – receiving information very quickly, as if a full story came to you in a condensed form

♥ **Tasting, Smelling** – actually tasting or smelling substances

I typically receive visual stories and knowing information. I might hear words and phrases, but often correlate them together. I also experience emotions, but often have to ask specific questions in order to receive these. Here are some examples of readings I've done that involve various forms of receiving:

Visually: I was talking to a dog in England and he clearly showed me his kitchen and his bed beside a staircase that was going up to the family's one-and-a-half-story farmhouse. He even showed me the tile on the floor. He also showed me their backyard with a fence line and a gate leading out to a field where he went for walks, but I had a knowing that it wasn't part of their land – perhaps a park or crown land. When I described this from my home in Canada the dog's person couldn't believe the accuracy.

Hearing: I was doing a reading on a horse and heard, "I am such a good boy." He repeated this throughout the reading. I confirmed with the horse's person that she continually tells him, "You are such a good boy," because he really was a perfect horse and had absolutely no problematic behaviors.

Feeling: My most profound feeling communication happened one evening at a farm, where I was walking up the aisle of the barn. I went up to a mare named Chase, who was standing in the corner of the stall. Her emotions hit me very strongly. I asked her if she wanted to share, and then I began to cry uncontrollably. Horses can't cry and she needed me to help her release all her sorrow. Her person had moved to Costa Rica and left Chase behind, as she was well over twenty years old and would not have made the trip very well.

Chase missed her person terribly. She felt abandoned and didn't want to live. I told Chase that her person loved her more than anything because Chase was her first horse and she'd had her since she was a baby. She wanted so badly to take Chase, but the trip was too long and hard and she felt it was the best to leave her there. I told Chase that her person would understand her grief and that she would want Chase to try to love the new person. I told her she needed to keep up her strength and drink and eat. We had a nice hug and then she went over to her water, took a big drink, and started to eat her hay. I was told later that Chase had been in a state of depression and was off her food and water, but after talking to me she was okay again.

Tasting, Smelling: A woman who came for a visit did a reading on my mare, Aurora. She asked Aurora what she liked to eat and distinctly got the taste and smell of molasses. She could also see the food and described it as "crumbly." The only food I was giving Aurora with molasses was beat pulp and I knew she didn't really love that. I showed the woman the food that she was getting and she said, "No, that's not it."

I then remembered that when I had her boarded at the old farm, she use to get sweet feed, which is a grain formula with oats, corn, and molasses. I had stopped giving her sweet feed a couple years back when she was pregnant and had her put on maternity food. I hadn't realized how much she loved sweet feed.

Asking Questions

There are some general questions you can ask animals to start communicating with them. I like to start with a few of these and then open it up to whatever the animal wants to tell me. I usually end with the last two.

General Questions:

1.   *Tell me about yourself.* This will start a flood of information that can lead you to further questions. If not much is coming then start with specifics.

2.   *What is your personality like?*

3.   *What do you like?*

4.   *What do you dislike?* This and the "like" question often provide specific answers that are undeniable.

5.   *What is your favorite activity?*

6.   *What is unique about you?*

7.   *Do you have a job? What is it?*

8.   *Where do you sleep?*

9.   (For cats) *Do you go outside?*

10. *Show me your home.*

11. *Tell me about your people.*

12. *What is your favorite food? Can you send me the taste or smell?*

13. *Is there anything you want to tell your person?*

14. *Is there anything you want to ask me, or your person?*

When practicing, it is best to try to get specific answers from the animal to help verify the results and prove to yourself that you are really exercising animal communication.

Prepare to Connect

We will now tie together the concepts and information received so far, so you can begin to connect and communicate with animals.

1. **Slow down** – The first important step is to slow your brain down to the Alpha state (relaxed awareness). This can be done by deep breathing exercises and relaxing every part of your body.

2. **Connect to Universal Energy** – this is done by bringing down white light into the top of your head and opening your crown chakra. Visualize the opening and the connection.

3. **Open your energy fields/chakras** – Bring the energy down through your body, activating each chakra. This raises the vibrations of your own subatomic particles (photon light), which increases your telepathic abilities.

4. **Ground yourself** – Send energy out through your aura and down through your feet into Mother Earth to ground yourself. Visualize roots growing out from your feet. At first, this process can take ten minutes or more to really get the most out of it. Over time, you will learn to do it in less time (even

seconds) by thinking the words "relax and connect," and if you work at it hard enough, you'll be able to remain in that connected state at all times.

Connecting for the first time will often bring on emotions. This is completely normal and healthy. You may feel joy or sadness; some will want to cry, and some will just feel like they have come back home. You may also experience headaches when doing this for the first few times, which happened to me. I later realized that re-opening my third eye and activating it was causing the headaches. Just like the start of a physical fitness program, when you have some aches and pains the next day, but it is all good. The headaches will quickly go away as you keep practicing.

It is also important to feel your own body, do a scan of what your body feels like, and notice your own emotions and aches or pains. When you connect to an animal you will know if the feelings or physical sensations you are sensing are coming from them or coming from you.

Connect to the Animal

Once you are in the relaxed state and connected to the universal energy, you are ready to connect with an animal.

1.   State the animal with whom you would like to communicate, and include as much information as possible to ensure it is the correct animal. Think of it as a phone call—you need to have the exact number to connect. You cannot just say, "I want to talk to Rover", as it is too vague. For readings over a distance, look at a picture, if you have one, and state the animal's name, and the animal's person's name. For example, you might say, "I would like to talk to Wulf, whose person is Ingrid Brammer at The Oasis Farm."

2. Open your heart and send the animal love. This ensures a connection to the animal. Visualize a stream of love coming from your heart connecting to theirs, or simply state the intention to connect your heart to theirs.

3. Ask for permission to talk to the animal.

4. Begin to communicate. Ask questions, and be open to receiving thoughts, visions, words, etc.

5. Record all that you receive, and do not censor. Trust that it is all coming from the animal for a reason. Ask more questions if some things are not clear.

6. When you are finished, thank the animal for communicating.

7. Disconnect your heart connection. You can do this by visualizing the connection disconnecting or simply state the intention to disconnect.

Interpreting Information

When receiving information intuitively, it will often be very quick and happen instantly. This flash of information is a clear sign that it came from the animal. Sometimes the information can seem strange; this, too, is a good sign and must be written down. If it is something you definitely wouldn't have thought up yourself, this is confirmation that it is coming from the animal. If you receive very obvious answers, like the cat hates baths, write it down too, because it may be something the animal just experienced and is still vivid in its mind.

Each person has a history of life experiences that can sometimes hamper what we believe we may be getting from the animals. It is important to begin the communication with a clear mind and write down everything exactly as you see, sense, hear, or feel it.

Early in my practice, I did a reading on a cat and the visual that appeared was my own living room. The setting wasn't relevant to the message that wanted to come across. There was a man in the living room who turned the TV on very loudly, and the cat ran out of the room because he didn't like the loud noise. The man also spoke loudly, and the cat would stay away from him.

There could be many interpretations of this scene, depending on the persons personal experience. My interpretation at that time was that the man must be yelling, possibly out of anger, when he raised his voice. The anger and yelling came out of my *mind*, not my *intuition*. All that I really picked up was that he spoke loudly. For the reading, I simply put that the cat didn't like loud voices, and that he preferred women to men.

The cat's person replied back to me as follows: *Your comments on Eddie were of particular interest and mostly right on the mark. My husband has a hearing problem and he just recently got a hearing aid that works for him. Prior to that he had a habit of playing the television rather loud—hence the loud voices that disturbed Eddie. He got so he would leave the room when the TV came on.*

I did not have any history or experience with people with hearing problems. However, I had been around angry people who raised their voices, so my interpretation was completely wrong.

I learned two valuable lessons in that reading. 1) Do not interject your own thoughts into what is being sent. Simply write down the facts you get. 2) Sometimes the visual may be in familiar places and have no relevance to the message.

You can also pick up symbols. Simply write down what you are receiving and ask questions that may help you figure them out, or ask the animal's person to help figure them out. I had one student do a reading on my dog Elmo and she received the picture of Daisies. I then told her that I had spent the summer planting a garden and had many Daisies and Daisy like flowers and Elmo spent the summer at my side while I planted. He enjoyed that.

Be the Animal Method

At times, it can be difficult to receive information from some animals and it may be necessary to try another approach. One method worth trying is similar to Gestalt Therapy, used by psychotherapists, who ask their clients to work through a relationship by playing both sides of the conversation. Usually, two chairs are set up; the client will sit in one chair and relate his issues as himself, and then move to the other chair and respond from the other person's perspective.

In animal communication you ask the animal a question and then *sit in the animal's place* to see, feel, hear, or know the answer. You place your consciousness inside the animal and actually feel what it is like to have fur, four feet, and see from the animal's perspective. You can often get deeper answers this way.

I used this method one day with my cat, Abby. Like my other cats, she disappears during the day when sleeping, but she never sleeps in the same place. I often have to look everywhere and sometimes find her in strange places, like my linen closet. I talked to her one day and saw through her own eyes, from *her* perspective that she gets excited and thinks, "Hmm, where can I hide today?" I realized that she makes a game out of it. She loves it and finds it intriguing and fun. I actually felt the emotions of excitement and intrigue. I felt like I wanted to slink down and crouch around silently and try to be invisible. I felt like I was playing hide and seek. It wasn't until I used this method that I understood how much she loved this part of her day.

Exercises

Here are some exercises to practice sending and receiving messages with your animal companion.

- ♥ Sit quietly and send a message to your animal. Ask her what she wants to do. She may get excited and come over. Open your intuition and receive the messages the animal is sending you. If it is something you can do, such as play ball or go for a walk, then comply. If it is a horse, ask him before you ride what he wants to work on or do that day. Listen for the messages and be prepared to consent to the activity if possible. If he tells you he wants to graze and not ride at all, but you do, a little negotiation might be in order.

♥ Sit quietly and just send love to your animal companion. See what comes back to you. Ask your animal questions and see what s/he says back. Write down whatever comes to you.

Attunement Exercise

In my classes, I take my students through an attunement exercise to prepare them to communicate for the first time. I provide a daily meditation to my students in the form of a CD or downloadable MP3, depending if the class is on-site, web based, or my home study program.

As it is best to do this exercise as a guided meditation, have someone read it to you while you close your eyes and follow along. Alternatively, you can record it and listen to the playback again with your eyes closed.

We will begin the meditation by taking deep breaths. Close your eyes and breathe in deeply; hold for a couple of seconds and release, slowly. As you release the breath, feel all the tension coming out of your body. You are becoming more and more relaxed. Notice all of the tension disappearing with each breath.

Inhale again; hold for a few seconds, and release, relaxing every part of you. Each breath brings you to a point of deeper relaxation. As you breathe in, feel the breath enter every cell of your body, bringing relaxation and peace.

Take a final deep inhalation, breathing in the calm and loving energy. Hold . . . and release.

Now, visualize, sense, or feel a brilliant white light coming down from the source of all energy. It shines down over you, filling, clearing, and protecting your entire aura.

Now, open your crown chakra at the top of your head and allow the white light to enter as you activate your universal connection.

The white light travels down and comes to your third eye, located between your brows. The third eye chakra now opens in the front and back of your head with the brilliant white light. Your intuition is now activated.

The light now moves down to your throat chakra, which opens in the front and back of your neck, activating your communication.

The white light continues down to reach your heart center. The white light is now purifying the front and back of the heart chakra, activating your love and compassion, to allow you to communicate feelings and emotions.

The white light now moves down to your solar plexus chakra, above the navel. This chakra is now open and has given you the power and will to communicate with animals.

The white light now moves to your sacral chakra, located below the navel, activating the flow the energy for the desire to communicate with animals.

The white light arrives at your root chakra, located at the base of your spine. As your root chakra opens, the white light continues down your legs and you begin to grow roots that extend down through Mother Earth, grounding you. You are connected to the universal energy, completing and harnessing the flow of energy.

You are now connected to your psychic ability to communicate with animals.

Any time you want to return to this connected state, simply breathe in and think the words, "relax and connect" and you will return to this calm, connected state.

Every day, you will get better and better at communicating with animals. You will listen with your inner ears, and see with your mind's eye. You will have a sense of knowing that will come from the animals and your higher self. Trust this process.

When communicating with animals, you must always respect them by asking, first, for permission, and always thank them for sharing with you. Animal communication must always be done with the best intentions and with love and compassion.

Say to yourself, "I have the ability to communicate telepathically with animals." Repeat these words. "I have the ability to communicate telepathically with animals."

Now, visualize, feel, or sense yourself communicating with animals.

I will leave you for a few minutes to enjoy this feeling, and when I speak again, it will not startle you.

We will begin to come back now to the present moment, slowly. Begin to move your fingers and toes and bring yourself back. When you are ready, open your eyes.

Animal Communication
Practice Exercise

I will now provide you with your first practice intuitive reading with one of my horses. You can use the meditation CD or the meditation from the previous chapter to get into the relaxed and connected state. I have the steps summarized below for you. There is an answer page at the end of the book which tells you all about "Wulf" to see if you picked up accurate information.

Prepare yourself to communicate:
"Relax and Connect."
1. Slow down with deep breathing.

2. Connect to universal energy.

3. Open your energy centers / chakras.

4. Ground yourself.

Communicate
5. Ask to connect to Wulf, whose person is Ingrid Brammer at The Oasis Farm. (You can also refer to him by his nickname, Wulfy.)

6. Open your heart and connect by sending him love.

7. Ask Wulf for permission to talk to him.

8. Begin to communicate by asking questions.

9. Record all that you receive, and do not censor. Trust that it is all coming from the animal for a reason. Ask more questions if some things are not clear.

10. Thank Wulf for communicating when you are finished

11. Disconnect your heart connection from Wulf.

WULFY

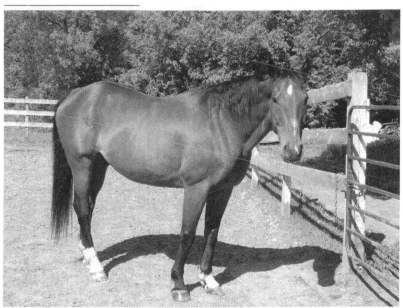

Registered Name: Mozart, however, he goes by his barn name, Wulf, or Wulfy. Born January 27, 1987. Color: Bay. Breed: Appendix (Quarter Horse / Thoroughbred cross).

For answers refer to Appendix C: Exercise Answer Sheet

Section 3:
Using and Expanding your New Skills

Inaccuracies and Why They Happen

When communicating with animals, it is important to realize that accuracy can vary from day to day. Your own state of mind, physical condition, and stress level can all influence the outcome. The state of the animal is also a key aspect. Lost, scared, or hurt animals may not be transmitting accurate information to you. Even professional animal communicators have "off" days. On average, eighty to ninety percent accuracy is what you want to strive for. Validating what we get from an animal is challenging, so getting a real percentage for accuracy can be difficult.

As I've stated before, the most common reason for inaccuracies is your own logical mind—it simply gets in the way. Try to clear your mind, and if there is doubt in what you are getting, or you feel that you are inserting your own thoughts into the reading, then ask the animal more questions to get a clearer message.

The animal could be sending you inaccurate answers that he truly believes are correct. I was once talking to a horse named "Boss," and I asked him how old he was. I clearly heard, "I think I am eleven." It was so clear that I knew it had to be right. When I confirmed with his person, she laughed and said, "No, he is twenty-two years old." She then told me that she got him when he was eleven, and for the longest time when friends and family would meet him, they would ask her how old he was, and she would always say, "I think he is eleven." That was all he knew.

When I was first learning, my accuracy on age was only about fifty percent, so I started asking for the age up front to avoid the confusion. My theory on age is that some animals don't know. It isn't relevant to them as they live in the moment, day to day. The ones that do know age know it from their people.

Inaccuracies can also happen when you know too much about the animal beforehand. The animal's person may have told you her side of the story, which may skew your logical mind and block the perception of opposing information that may come in. I only ask for the picture, name, sex, and age of the animal, and nothing else.

Intuitive Blocks and How to Overcome Them

Everyone has the ability to turn on their intuition. Depending on many factors, this process can be very quick, or it may take months to get results. If you find you are not receiving information, it could be due to a number of reasons.

In Lynne McTaggart's book, *The Intention Experiment*, she discusses some scientific reasons why we may have better psychic days than others. She cites the earth's geomagnetic activity as one aspect that can have an effect on our psychic abilities. She states:

> *During days of geomagnetic calm, spontaneous instances of telepathy or clairvoyance are more likely to occur and remote viewing accuracy is more likely to improve.*

Your belief system may be playing a role. We all have beliefs we live by that are buried deep inside ourselves. I often call these the "tapes" we play in our head. They may be the words from our childhood that our parents or teachers may have told us, such as, "You can't do that," or, "That's not real." It can also be your own critic running rampant in your mind. Another belief that you may have adopted is that psychic activity is wrong. This was and still is a common thought in some cultures. It is important to listen to these tapes when they come up, to try to figure out where they came from and then let them go. Tell yourself the opposite message everyday in your meditations.

Negative thinking is a big reason why intuition may be blocked. If you think positively and expect results, you will be amazed at how your animal communication will start working. Reverse all your negative thoughts into positive statements and repeat them to yourself *daily*. These affirmations will change your attitude in no time.

Energy blocks are a key factor in inhibiting animal communications. Our energies need to flow in our bodies, and if you have blockages they will stop intuitive activity, and can also cause illness and disease. If you believe you have blocked energy, the best thing to do is to start a daily meditation practice. Bring the universal energy in, and open your chakras. Listen to the messages your body is giving you in your meditations. Various alternative health care practices can be utilized to speed up the process, such as energy healing, or Reiki. Oftentimes the problem is due to emotional blocks that may need some help from a life coach, a counselor or therapist.

Stress is a huge factor that will cause us to shut down our intuitive side. Physical activity is the best means to release stress. This can be complemented by exercises that will calm your mind and relax your body, such as a daily meditation. If stress is a daily occurrence due to your lifestyle, think about what can be done to eliminate some of the causes of stress in your life.

Diet is also an important factor here. High-sugar intake, excess caffeine, drugs, and alcohol can negatively affect our intuitive abilities. Conversely, a healthy diet and exercise help to open intuitive skills.

Performance anxiety is another issue that can cause a shutdown to occur. If you know you will have to tell others about what you are receiving and you feel silly about sharing the answers, take the pressure off yourself and lighten up. Some inaccuracies will happen; don't expect perfection. Try to stay positive and expect the best from the communication.

Trying too hard is another common issue that beginners often run into. We are so eager to start receiving information that our logical mind takes over and causes us to stress unnecessarily. We need to learn to quiet down the rational side and relax. Rather than have a sharp mind, we need to have soft inner eyes to flow with what comes in.

Working With Your Own Animals

When talking with your own animals, it is hard to keep your mind and thoughts clear. Also, you do not have someone to verify the results with you, so it is a challenge to trust your intuition.

When working with our own animals we often want to be able to have an intuitive conversation at any given moment. With lots of practice you will get to that stage. Since we are in tune with our own animals, and we often have a heart connection with them all the time, it is not always necessary to go through the full exercise to connect. However, as a beginner, until you get to the point where you can have a ready mind in an instant, you need to prepare yourself by slowing down, opening up, and tuning in the same way you would when practicing with animals you do not know. Try using the *Be the Animal* method discussed earlier.

Over time, you will begin to feel and know the difference between messages that come from your own head and those that come from outside of you.

To start, practice sending your animals information. Talk to them out loud and explain things. They will already know what you are saying because they are tuned in, but this is a good lesson in practicing your communication skills with them. Speak to them as if they are another person, as equals. Over time you can do this silently and send pictures, feelings, and thoughts.

There are times when you just know your animals are trying to tell you something. You are right, they are! These are your first intuitive messages, and you received them. They may be due to body language as they sit and stare at you. Take the time to listen to what they are trying to say. Ask questions, and ask them to send you clear, simple messages. They could be in the form of a picture or a feeling, if that is easier for you. Ask them to send you a question that you can answer. Do not try to solve behavioral issues from the beginning; just try to keep the lines open, and send questions that are simple, like, "What is your favorite color?"

To keep your animal companions happy, keep them informed. If you have to leave for any period of time, tell them where you are going and when you will be back. They will understand. When I have to travel, I tell my Bichon, Halle, who is very close to me, that I have to go for two sleeps and I will be back. I tell her that she will be with her aunt (my daughter) and she will have fun and be well taken care of. When I am away, I connect to her before bed each night and send her love. Distance does not matter; we connect the same way and she receives it. You can even do this if you only have to be gone for a few hours.

For dog lovers, I highly recommend Cesar Millan's books, and his TV program, *The Dog Whisperer*, to learn more about dog psychology. Cesar's advice is to stay calm and assertive, and be the pack leader. Dogs become balanced and happy when we are in charge. Learning to communicate telepathically helps us to realize that we are sending messages to our animals, and we want to be clear in what we are sending. You can help animals work through any worries, fears, or issues they have, so they become more secure and balanced.

Animals come into our lives for a reason. Sometimes they find us and sometimes we find them, but regardless, I believe that it is just meant to be. You can ask your companion some questions that will help to deepen your relationship:

- ♥ What is your purpose in my life?
- ♥ What is my purpose in your life?

Helping Animals

Working with Behavioral Issues

Animals act out for various reasons. The first step in understanding what might be going on is to rule out any physical issues first. Animals that start acting fearful, aggressive, or destructive may be acting out due to a physical problem.

Oftentimes, when horses start behaving badly, it can be that pain is causing them to react without control. One common issue is tooth pain. If you suspect this to be the situation, have an equine dentist look at your horse. Poor-fitting tack is also a common occurrence that can lead to back pain and sore spots. Ensure that saddles fit properly and do not have pressure points that will cause pain. Try equine massage therapists to help stiff and sore horses.

There are also physical reasons why dogs and cats might behave badly, which could include having accidents in the house. Urinary tract infections, or crystals in the bladder, can be deadly for male cats. Unfortunately, I experienced this firsthand when my male cat, Sylvester, began urinating on the carpet in front of me. I wasn't aware of this condition in cats, nor did I realize the gravity of the situation. He passed away within two days of when the accidents began. Other internal pain or gastric problems can also appear as behavioral issues.

As animals are emotional beings, just like humans, their behavior often has an emotional or mental basis. Still, their issues can be resolved even if they have been occurring for a long time.

Always begin your animal communication with love and compassion. Once connected to the animal, begin to ask questions that may reveal the reasons for their conduct, such as:

1. Why you are behaving this way?
2. How does this behavior make you feel?
3. Is there something physical that is bothering you?
4. Is there something you need to help you?
5. What can I do for you?

Show the animal what you want him to do and how good behavior looks.

I once helped a cat who was very upset that the kitty litter was never clean, and had refused to use it. I mentioned this to the cat's person and after keeping it very clean, the cat started to use the litter box again.

During the winter, when the snow slides off the riding arena roof, it can send the horses into a bolt down the arena, leaving the rider hanging on for dear life.

One winter, my stallion, Diestro, was particularly spooked and I kept telling him that he was safe and nothing would happen. It did not make any difference, as the fear was too strong. I then decided to change my tactic, and told him that his job was to keep *me* safe, and that when he bolted it was dangerous for me. After that, he was very calm and slow when I rode him.

One day, my daughter came home from college for a visit and went to the barn with me. I hadn't told her about my conversation with Diestro. Before I started to ride, I telepathically told Diestro, "I want you to be a good boy and keep me safe," as I always did. As I was riding around the arena, my daughter said, "Hey Mom, guess what Diestro just said to me, 'Aren't I a good boy, I am keeping her safe.' I was absolutely thrilled to hear this. I then told her exactly what I had been trying that winter and how that confirmation was amazing.

Some behavioral issues need to be resolved through a training program. Cesar Millan's books and TV programs are amazing for dog rehabilitation. They guide people through a process to solve behavior issues. Pat Parelli's show and other natural horsemanship programs are available for horse owners. Never rule out a professional trainer to help.

We can ask our children to keep their rooms clean and pick up after themselves because that is good behavior, but generally, it isn't that easy. Additional work, negotiation, and compromises are often required. The same can be true for animals.

Finding a Lost Animal

Looking for a lost animal can be very emotional for all parties involved. The animal will very often be confused and scared and can send some mixed messages about his whereabouts and circumstances.

It can even be harder for people who are looking for their own animal. Make sure you exercise conventional measures, such as calling animal shelters and veterinarians, going door-to-door in your neighborhood, and putting up posters. With your new skill, you will now also have the means to tune in and try to talk to your lost animal. If you get confusing messages, try the "be the animal" method to see if you can *see* through their eyes at their surroundings. When we look from the animal's eyes and see the area they are in, this is also known as "remote viewing."

Try asking some of these questions:

1. Where are you? Can you describe your surroundings?
2. Are you indoors or outdoors?
3. Is it cold or warm? Is it dark or light? Is it wet or dry?
4. Are you safe?

5. Are you injured or sick?

6. Do you have food and water?

7. How did you get there? Can you show me the path you took?

8. How can I find you?

9. Why did you leave?

Sometimes animals leave for a reason, and it is always important to find out why. There may be some solutions to the animal's issues that will bring her home on her own.

You can also ask for some guidance in your dreams. When going to sleep at night ask your lost animal to come to you in your dreams to help provide more information.

In Lynne McTaggart's book, *The Field,* she explains the many tests the CIA did with remote viewing. The CIA used psychics to view the enemy territory to help with tactical procedures. Prior to actually using the information during warfare, they went through many studies and trials to prove that the ability was valid. In one study, the remote viewer saw a building with a swimming pool and two water tanks. However, they compared the actual site with the viewer's description, and there were no water tanks. They thought the experiment was a failure, until they received a picture of the site fifty years prior and the two water tanks were clear and exactly as described.

When tuning into a lost animal it is very important to ask for present information. Ask "the universal energy" to give you exact information in the present time. Ask precise questions to narrow in, if possible.

I once had a call from a woman who had lost her male cat. He had been gone for a couple of days and her family had looked everywhere. They had posted "missing" signs and were worried sick. I tuned into the cat and I saw him walking down the street on the sidewalk of a sub-division. Then he came to a park where he ran across to a forest. I saw him there hiding among some trees that were on the ground. He was very scared and hungry and thirsty.

I told the cat's people and they said they knew of a park down the road that had a forest beside it. I was very happy to hear that they went to the forest and after repeatedly calling out, the cat came running to them. This was a very rewarding experience that had a wonderful ending.

Not all missing animal stories have a happy ending. One question you will have to ask the animal is whether it is still in its physical body. Animals may not realize that they have died, and may still want to come home. They may be confused, and in that situation it can be difficult to get a clear message. If you do not get a clear "yes" or "no," try these exercises to help clarify.

- ♥ Connect with the animal and sense if the animal is grounded or if s/he feels like s/he is weightless.
- ♥ Visualize the animal in body and in spirit. Have the two images side by side in your mind. Ask which form the animal is in, and ask one of the images to light up.
- ♥ Use the "be the animal" method and check if the animal is breathing and has a pulse.

We hope never to have to utilize this method, but it is, nevertheless, something we need to understand how to do.

In the summer of 2009, I had the unfortunate firsthand experience of having a lost cat. Our fifteen-year-old tabby, Tasha, went missing. We started to look for her later in the afternoon, until dark. I tuned in to Tasha throughout the day and received her journey. I saw where she went and I followed the path through the forest. It was dense with bush and overgrowth and difficult to see any tracks. As it got dark I tuned in again and told her to hide in a safe place because there were coyotes around.

I asked several of my students to tune in and help if they wanted to, and we had many similar readings that helped with the search.

The next morning, I tuned in again and I tried "be the animal." I distinctly saw the view looking down from above. I felt that she had moved on and was looking down as spirit. I did not want to believe that and I quickly asked if she was up in a tree looking down. Although we proceeded to look for her for another week, we never did find Tasha.

I learned a great deal from my own unfortunate experience. I had reached out to my students and other professional animal communicators that I knew to help with the search at the time. Some confirmed my feelings of her passing on, while others continued to see her alive and in different places.

What I came to realize is that when we communicate with animals, we are connecting to the quantum world, so time is not relevant. The visions we see and information we get may not be in the present. I believe that everyone who tried to connect with Tasha received valid information, but it wasn't necessarily current information. This concept makes finding lost animals very difficult.

Working with Health Issues

The real advantage to animal communication comes from helping the animals. Communicating with a sick animal is not to replace conventional care by a qualified veterinarian, but rather to complement and assist with diagnosis and treatment.

To communicate with a sick animal, tune in just as you've been taught. Ask the animal for his symptoms and what specifically is causing the discomfort. Ask him for his past history and any illnesses that may have contributed to his current state. Once you have a clear picture from the animal, talk to the animal's person to validate the information and to understand it better.

If clairsentience is a strong method for you, and you believe you need to feel the actual discomfort to understand it better, then you can ask to feel the discomfort. You have the ability to block the pain or discomfort by simply asking the animal to tell you what he is feeling, and by asking not to *experience* the actual feelings yourself. There is no need to take on the energy of the sickness either way.

For people that have stronger clairvoyance mode, a more advanced method is to do a body scan. This method is to visualize the animal and ask for the area to light up or show itself. Scan the body for energy darkness to help pinpoint the area. You can picture in your mind the animal as a holograph and visualize them on a turntable and as they turn look into their body in various levels. Start with the skeletal structure, then add the circulatory system, then add the organs. Keep adding layers of muscle, tissues, etc., and sense or pick up knowing information from what you see.

Another method is to enter the body as if you were a small microorganism and as you look around inside you can see areas that may have illness or disease. For your own animals trust your own intuition and feelings as we are so close to our own animals we often know when they are not acting 100% normal. Clue into your first feelings and take the time to tune in and ask, feel or see what is wrong. Ask them what they need to be better.

When I was first learning animal communication, I was working with a woman named Lorna, whose dog, Caleigh, was experiencing small moments of pain. She would freeze up, clearly in pain, and then relax and act normal. The vet thought it was gastric, so she was put on special food, but it wasn't helping.

I tuned into Caleigh one afternoon and clearly got the impression that the right hip area was where the pain was coming from. I gently told Lorna, as I wasn't sure how she would react to someone using intuitive communications. Luckily, she was open-minded and after taking Caleigh for an MRI and various other tests they found a pinched nerve in her back, which affected her hip. She has since had some arthritis and other ailments, but is a happy and very loved dog, nonetheless.

I worked with another dog named Annie, a two year old yellow lab. I was told that she was limping and the veterinarians were not able to pin-point the problem, after x-rays and other examinations. She did have another appointment scheduled for an ultrasound but was getting concerned at the accumulating costs.

When I tuned into Annie, I immediately knew it was her front left leg that had the issue. I then tuned into the feelings and received a tingling tightness in my left neck, up behind my ear and down to below my ear lobe, then down through the shoulder area. I could feel a dull aching with a tight stiffness in this area. The visual was very clear. I could see the top view of Annie, there was a hot, inflamed red energy through the entire section, starting behind the ear and going down the neck through her shoulder. I received a knowing that it was in the muscles or tendons, and that massage and energy healing would help Annie heal.

After I tuned in, I reviewed a diagram of canine muscle structure and found the exact name of the muscle that I visualized and told Annie's person what I found. She continued with the ultrasound and the specialist confirmed Annie had tendonitis in her left front shoulder. She was thrilled with the results and commented on that the depth of information was remarkable as I had not even seen Annie in person.

Sometimes your animal communicates with you in your dreams. If you have a dream that involves your animal be sure to listen to it and try to understand the meaning. Dreams can either be symbolic or very straightforward.

Before I had my own farm, I had my horses at various places. When I retired my older horse, I had to move him from the training farm, where he had always been, to another farm that was taking care of older, retired horses. I tried to visit him every month or more, but at this time, it had been about six weeks since I had seen him.

I'd had a dream that he was skin and bones, and starving. I awoke in panic. I was scheduled to go away on a business trip that day, so I left early for the airport and took a detour to go see him. To my dismay, he had lost a lot of weight and was, in fact, very thin. The other horses were not thin, so I was worried that he was ill or having physical issues.

When I returned from my trip two days later, my husband and I went back to see him, he appeared even thinner, so we decided to remove him from there. I made some calls and arranged to bring him to another farm, close to me, so I could find the reason for his condition and help him to return to health. I am happy to say that he is now in fantastic health and enjoying his retirement at The Oasis, with a new purpose: to help teach people to communicate with animals.

The subject of health issues and healing using energy methods is something that I am passionate about. I will be writing a second book dedicated to this subject and provide additional methods on how to scan for health issues.

Death and Dying

With all the great joys of having animals, unfortunately, there comes a time when you may need to make a very difficult choice whether to help them end their life. It is always the hope that our animal companions leave us peacefully in their sleep without any illness or suffering. This isn't always reality. We are often more humane to our animal friends than we are with our own kind when we help them move on.

It isn't a decision that you take lightly and this is a particularly good time to communicate with your animal directly or call upon a professional animal communicator if that is easier for you. The decision is ultimately between the animal and her person, and should be based on her current condition and quality of life. If she is suffering or in pain in any way and there is no chance for the suffering to end, then it is humane to assist in the best, most peaceful way possible.

When communicating with your animal, ask her clearly what s/he wants. Listen and trust that you are receiving from your animal. Tell her to give you a sign when the time comes.

Talk to her beforehand and tell her how you feel about her, and having shared her life with you. If you believe in reincarnation and want her to return one day, you can tell her that also.

There are many organizations that provide assistance with grief and loss and can assist in this difficult time.

I often get people asking me to help with their decision. They typically want to know if the animal is ready, how he is feeling, and if he is in pain. I do not feel it is right to help make the decision, but what I can do is talk to the animal. I can ask simple questions with regard to the animal's quality of life, such as how he is feeling, and whether he is in pain or suffering. This information can assist the animal's person to make an informed decision.

Working with Animals in Spirit

I have found that connecting with animals once they are in spirit helps the person's grief process. The animal's person can see that their companion is at peace and often running through the fields being happy.

To communicate with animals in spirit, you use the same process of connection and communication as when they are alive. The animal's energy and consciousness, or soul, is still part of the collective consciousness.

We had to make the difficult decision for our beloved Elmo to put him to rest, and when the time came he went very peacefully at our home. He now has a lovely spot on our farm where we visit him. I will be putting a daisy garden in the area.

In my classes, I have asked the students to connect and report on their conversations with Elmo, and the results have been very accurate. To practice speaking with animals that have passed on, I have provided another exercise on the following page.

Animal Communication Practice Exercise

You can use the meditation CD, or the previous one, to get into the relaxed and connected state. I have the steps summarized below for you to reference. To see if you picked up accurate information, there is an answer page at the end of the book, which tells you all about Elmo.

Prepare yourself to communicate:
"Relax and connect."
1. Slow down using deep breathing.
2. Connect to universal energy.
3. Open your energy centers / chakras.
4. Ground yourself.

Communicate
5. Ask to connect to Elmo now in spirit, whose person was Ingrid Brammer at The Oasis Farm.
6. Open your heart and send him love.
7. Ask Elmo for permission to talk to him.

8. Begin to communicate, and ask questions the same as you would before.

9. Record all that you receive, and do not censor. Trust that it is all coming from the animal for a reason. Ask more questions if some things are not clear.

10. Thank Elmo for communicating when you are finished.

Elmo

September 17, 1995 – November 2, 2008
His breed is an English Springer Spaniel.
For Answers refer to- Appendix C: Exercise Answer Sheet

Appendix A: Quick Reference Sheet – Animal Communication

Preparation

Prepare yourself to communicate with an animal. Find a quiet spot, close your eyes, and follow the connection steps:

1. Slow down. The first important step is to slow down your brain to the Alpha state, which is one of awareness and relaxation.

2. Connect to Universal Energy. This is done by bringing white light down into the top of your head and opening your crown chakra.

3. Bring the energy down through your body, activating each chakra.

4. Send energy out through your aura and down through your feet into Mother Earth to ground yourself. Think of, or visualize, roots growing from your feet.

Begin Communication

1. Always start by asking to communicate with a specific animal by name, and if you have a picture, look at it, or visualize it as you close your eyes. Mention any other information you may have about the animal, such as his person's name, to ensure that you are connecting to the correct animal. Like dialing a phone number, you need to request specific information and your intentions will be met.

2. Send the animal love from your heart to theirs.

3. Ask the animal for permission to speak with him. You will get a feeling of "yes" or "no," or a specific word. Always respect the animal's privacy and wishes.

4. Ask the animal some questions, such as, "What is your favorite food, where do you sleep, what makes you special, or what is your job?"

5. Record all that you receive, and do not censor. Trust that it is all coming from the animal for a reason. Ask more questions if some things are not clear.

6. Thank the animal for communicating when you are finished.

7. Disconnect the heart connection.

Review Questions

1. *Tell me about yourself.* This will start a flood of information that can lead you to further questions. If not much is coming then start with specifics.

2. *What is your personality like?*

3. *What do you like?*

4. *What do you dislike?* This and the "like" question often provide specific answers that are undeniable.

5. *What is your favorite activity?*

6. *What is unique about you?*

7. *Do you have a job? What is it?*

8. *Where do you sleep?*

9. (For cats) *Do you go outside?*

10. *Show me your home.*

11. *Tell me about your people?*

12. *What is your favorite food? Can you send me the taste or smell?*

13. *Is there anything you want to tell your person?*

14. *Is there anything you want to ask me, or your person?*

I usually end with the last two questions.

Appendix B: Exercises

Here are some exercises to practice sending messages to your animal companion.

- ♥ Think of something you admire in your companion and send the compliment to your animal, silently, in your mind. Know that it is received.

- ♥ Open your heart center and send love and compassion. See it being received.

- ♥ Send an image of a treat in your hand, and see your animal eating it. Once s/he comes over, give her the treat. If at first s/he is not listening, send the message telepathically, then out loud, then give it to her. Over time, s/he will come to you right away, with only the silent message.

- ♥ Without any physical or verbal messages, send a thought to your dog that it is time for a walk. Send the upbeat emotions typically related to walking and see if s/he comes to you. You do not need to be in the same room. Sit quietly. Send a picture of you getting ready, then leaving the house, and then doing what s/he typically does on his walk. Then take him for the walk.

♥   When going on your walk, visualize the route you are planning to take, send this message, and see if your dog turns before you.

♥   For any animal, take two bowls and put the exact same food in them. Send a message of which one the animal should go to and then put them both down, apart from each other. Let the animal choose one of the bowls. Try this everyday and switch the order around to see if the animal goes to the one you intended.

♥   When you are away from home, try sending messages to your companion that you are on your way back. Have someone at home notice if the animal responds in some way. Try coming home at different times of the day.

♥   Hide your dog's favorite toy when s/he is not looking. Then when s/he comes into the room, send her the picture of where the toy is and see if s/he finds it.

Here are some exercises to practice sending and receiving messages with your animal companion.

♥   Sit quietly and send a message to your animal and ask her what s/he wants to do. S/he may get excited and come over. Open your intuition and receive the messages the animal is sending you. If it is something you can do, such as play ball or go for a walk, then comply. If it is a horse, ask her before you ride what s/he wants to work on or do that day. Listen to the messages and be prepared to consent to the activity if possible. If s/he tells you s/he wants to graze and not ride at all, but you do, a little negotiation might be in order.

♥   Sit quietly and just send love to your animal companion. See what comes back to you. Ask him questions and see what s/he says back. Do this the same way you did in class with animals you didn't know. Write down whatever comes to you.

Appendix C: Exercise Answer Sheet

Wulf

1. Tell me about yourself
   - Retired, Was a school horse, children lesson horse, Cdn National Dressage Champion, Won competitions and loved it, Children would dress him up in costumes, He was Ingrid's partner for ~7 yrs and schoolmaster. Still is Ingrid's soul mate. Handsome.

2. What is your personality like?
   - Kind, sweet, caring, calm, head of the herd, responsible, understanding, playful, sense of humour, sensitive, deeply emotional, and very wise horse.

3. What do you like?
   - Loves to graze in the grass (Canada we only have 4 months of the year),
   - Mares (loves his women)

4. What do you dislike? Spurs

5. What is unique [special] about you?
   - Bombproof, very active throughout his life

- Sore feet, especially his right front foot (Navicular Disease)
- His color is Blue – halters, brushes, etc.

6. Do you have a job – what is it?
   - Helping people with Animal Communication, helping the younger horses (babysitter, teaches them how to socialize better)

7. Where do you sleep?
   - In summer in fields 24/7 but in the winter comes in barn at night. Tells people he likes deep straw, but we use pellets now.

8. Tell me about your people?
   - He often tells other students he loves Ingrid very much
   - Ingrid bought him when he was 11 and before that he was with her trainer for his whole life.

9. What is your favourite food? Can you send me the taste or smell?
   - Grass, apples, carrots, mints, Alfalfa
   - Eats Senior food and loves it, he gets glucosamine supplements

I will add additional information about Wulf so you can verify the information you received.

My trainer had had Wulf since he was four months old. I purchased him when he was eleven years old. He has only had two owners. During the first eleven years of his life, he was trained in the dressage discipline and used in the school for advanced riders. He won the Canadian National Dressage Championships at the basic level with one of the students.

I purchased him for his great training, but mostly for his great personality. He was considered "bombproof" and very solid and stable, ideal for a novice adult rider with fear. My two daughters were also taking lessons, so the three of us started to ride him. Eventually, I was the only one who rode him. He and I were partners for seven years as he taught me how to ride. He is a schoolmaster and was patient and forgiving as I learned.

Wulf was in a lot of competitions and always won the ribbons. He loved competing and putting on a show when being tested. He loved the pampering and the grooming, and getting his hooves polished and hair braided.

He was in the school before I bought him and was sometimes in summer camps, where kids would dress him up in costumes. He was always great with kids.

He loves his women! When put with mares, Wulf is very protective and obsessed with staying close to them. He has always been the head of the herd, at the top of the pecking order.

In his early teens, his feet started to bother him and he was diagnosed with *navicular*, a condition where there is pain in the hooves. His front feet were affected, particularly his front right foot. He'd had shoes on his front feet his whole life until he was retired. He is now barefoot. I retired him when he was about seventeen, as he was too sore to work.

Wulf was hurt and upset when I started to ride my Andalusian stallion, Diestro, and would watch us from the edge of the fence. During a financial situation, I was forced to move him to a retirement home where he was not happy, and lost a lot of weight. (See the story I mentioned earlier.)

His color is blue, and his halters and grooming materials are blue. He has had a blue or green blanket on in the winter his whole life, except for the last couple years because I want his hair to grow and the other horses always tear them off of him anyway. On really cold days, he gets a blanket.

Wulf has always been an easy keeper, but in his older age it has been hard to keep weight on him, so I give him senior feed every day, along with glucosamine and biotin for his feet. He loves apples, carrots, and mints.

He is my soul mate and has helped to illuminate me in ways I cannot even describe. Horses are so intuitive and connected to us. They bring happiness and oneness, and make us live in the moment. All my worries seem to go away when I am with him. Wulf has opened my eyes to a whole new world.

Elmo

Elmo was the perfect family dog, sweet and friendly. We adopted him when he was three years old. He'd been with a family that had small children who became allergic to him. During the summers, they had him living outside.

When we received him, we had him neutered. His eyes needed an operation, as they were inverted and had ulcers on them.

At that time, we lived in a waterfront home. Elmo loved to swim. He swam all summer and gathered rocks out of the water and brought them up on the shore. He stayed close to home and became a best friend to my two daughters during their childhood and teenage years.

Elmo liked to fetch balls and sticks when he was younger. He also liked to stand on the dock ladder and look at the fish in the lake; sometimes he tried to bite them. He went on walks through the farm fields adjacent to our home, then on *our* fields once we moved to the farm, and he loved it.

Elmo was a confident dog, very social, and kind. He would bark if someone came to the door, but would be happy to see them come in. He was very expressive, and would even say his name, "El-mo" when talking.

He did have some health issues, starting with a thyroid problem that required daily medication. That caused skin issues and sometimes he had sores on his belly. His hair stopped growing and what remained had been lightened by the sun.

Elmo went into kidney failure at age eleven and was on an IV and in critical condition for three days at the vet's office. We moved to the farm right around the same time. For the next two years he had some separation anxiety and didn't like to be alone. He didn't know how to be around the horses, so he would snap at them if they came close to smell him.

Eventually, he lost his hearing and some of his eyesight, but we worked closely with him to keep him safe. In the end, he had arthritis and lost the ability to move his hind end, but his heart was as big as always. Elmo was the best big dog I've ever had.

I loved and missed him so much that six months after his passing I purchased another English Springer Spaniel pup who has helped fill the hole in my heart. But Elmo will always hold a special place there.

Resources

Learning Their Language: Intuitive Communication with Animals and Nature by Marta Williams and D.V.M. Cheryl Schwartz

The Tao of Equus: A Woman's Journey of Healing and Transformation through the Way of the Horse by Linda Kohanov

Dogs That Know When Their Owners Are Coming Home: And Other Unexplained Powers of Animals by Rupert Sheldrake

The Secret Life of Plants by Peter Tompkins and Christopher Bird

The Biology of Belief: Unleashing the power of Consciousness, Matter and Miracles by Bruce Lipton, PH.D.

The Intention Experiment: Using Your Thoughts to Change Your Life and the World by Lynne McTaggart

The Field: The Quest for the Secret Force of the Universe by Lynne McTaggart

About the Author

Ingrid Brammer is an International Animal Communicator, FEEL (Facilitated Equine Experiential) Facilitator, Reiki Master and Quantum Touch Practitioner. She has trained extensively in intuitive studies, healing modalities and spiritual practices. Ingrid began teaching formal Intuitive Animal Communication Courses in 2009, and brings her years of experience, and the fundamental know how to others.